The ~~Beginner's~~ First-Novelist's

Guide to

William Essex

CLIMBING TREE BOOKS

First published 2022

Copyright © William Essex 2022

ISBN 978-1-909172-44-9

Published by
Climbing Tree Books Ltd, Falmouth, Cornwall, UK

www.climbingtreebookstore.com

Cover design and typesetting by Grace Kennard

All rights reserved. No reproduction without the prior
permission of the publisher.

I would like to dedicate this book to Melusie Evans,
who turned up unexpectedly half-way through my novel
Escape Mutation – A Journal of the Plague Years
and transformed it.

Also to Lucia Bradley, who isn't here yet – but
I'm pretty sure she's on her way.
She's going to be a real character.

Contents

Let's Start by Getting Started

Write down today's date. You've bought - or at least opened - a book on how to start your first novel. Let's find out how long it takes you to get started.*

The difficult part is not wanting to do it. You can want to write a novel and you can even plan to write a novel – and still end up not writing a novel. You can imagine yourself as a writer and you can see your novel clearly in your mind's eye – and still end up not writing a novel.

Only writing counts as writing.

That's the difficult part.

You have to *write* your novel.

So we will start with a writing exercise.

Write for me, please, a sentence of fiction.

This doesn't have to be the unimpeachably perfect opening sentence that you've been so stuck trying to find. Nor does it have to be a sentence that uniquely expresses a fundamental truth about the human condition.

* Procrastination is an issue here, but I'll get to that later.

It has to be yours. Original. Written by you.

Apart from that - anything. Any sentence of fiction. Make something up.

I'll wait.

Okay, so what's it going to be?

He sat staring at the words in front of him and trying to think up a sentence of fiction.

If you wrote that, and you are a *He*, okay, good enough. Just. [Extra points if you wrote a *He* sentence but you're not a *He*. Or vice-versa. Fiction is what we want here.]

Thank you.

The challenge now is to look at that first sentence and write the sentence that follows it. The second sentence. Then - I think you're ahead of me here - look at the first and second sentences together and write the third sentence. And stop on three (unless you want to continue, in which case, go right ahead).

You want three connected, consecutive sentences of fiction.

Important. Don't spend hours, or even minutes, on this. Make the second sentence a spontaneous follow-on from the first, and make the third a spontaneous follow-on from - yeah, you've got it.

He sat staring at the words in front of him and trying to think up a sentence of fiction. The writing really was the difficult part. So obvious now he thought about it.

Hmm. What we DON'T want here is a diary entry. We absolutely do NOT want a slice of real life.* This is an exercise in writing fiction. Making stuff up.

* If your whole plan is to write a lightly fictionalised version of your own life, ignore this.

8

From that short paragraph, you might have an idea of who *He* is, and you could probably make up some details of He's life. But ... it's as if I've taken myself to the gym but I'm only lifting the light weights.

He sat staring at the words in front of him and trying to think up a sentence of fiction. If he couldn't do this, he would know that the magic really was gone. His whole being depended on inventing the world around him, and yet today he was stuck in this dark featureless cavern and unable to write his way out of it.

For the purpose of this exercise, that's better. No, really.

I have a mental picture of *He* sitting at a fold-up table (where did that come from?) in his *dark featureless cavern*, and I'm fairly confident that if I wanted to do so, I could keep the story going. I'm curious about the idea of inventing the world with words - which fits in here, right?

I hope that you have three sentences in front of you now that are total fiction. I hope that they work as fiction for you, as my *He* in his *cavern* works for me - as the source of a mental picture that wasn't there before, that could be part of a bigger mental picture.

Your three sentences weren't Opening Sentences in any big, heavy, must-get-this-right sense, nor were they intended to be part of any novel you might be planning to write. You didn't - I hope - take too much trouble over them.

I don't think I can claim to have got you started - yet. But you've done something more than just write, I don't know, forty-ish words?

. What I hope you take from this exercise is the sense that you've lifted the curtain on a new fictional world. Just one corner of the curtain, and you can only see the little three-sentence bit that you've written, but - just look at the size of that curtain!

This is what you're capable of doing. With three sentences, you've written your way into a novel that you weren't even thinking of writing.

Repeat the exercise. Lift another curtain. Go wild. Lift another corner of the same curtain. Have fun. Make stuff up.

Then go back to the novel that you are thinking of writing, and write a sentence. Not an Opening Sentence. Just a sentence. Then another one.

And another one.

Have fun.

Where Does Planning Come into This?

You can plan. You'll need to plan. You can scribble notes to yourself, draw up timelines, use all the features on all the software programmes you can find to help you with your first novel.

But planning isn't the unfamiliar thing. You plan your day. You plan how you're going to get to work. Who's coming to your party. Whole areas of your brain are configured for planning.

So make a plan. Do what you know how to do. Do it before you write, or while you write, or both. Plan what to write, or fit what you've written already into a plan.

You might already have a fully developed plan for a big fat fantasy novel cycle (across twelve books) about a galaxy-wide clash of civilisations over who gets the mineral rights to the newly discovered alternate dimension.

Or you might have a vague idea that you could perhaps write a lightly fictionalised account of how it feels to be somebody like you living through times like these.

Or something in between. Or something else. There might be dragons in it.

Whatever your plan - if any - here's what matters.

Your plan is **positive**. It is **useful**.

It is infinitely **adaptable** and it is **whatever you want it to be**.

It will probably turn out to be lots of little plans scribbled to yourself as you go along. It will include word counts, ideas, odd sentences, snatches of dialogue, words with circles drawn around them, names, words with arrows to other words, print-outs, crossings-out, indecipherable scribbles added in the middle of the night.

Your plan might start in a fancy notebook, and it might look quite cool and creative for a while, but chances are, you will end up keeping it in a bag.

Your plan will make you smile.

Your plan **must** support your writing. It **must** make you happy. Your plan **must not** become a burden, an obligation, a reminder that you wrote something down and now can't find it. Your plan **must** be capable of adapting (changing) if (when) your writing takes you off in a wholly unexpected direction.

Make a plan that you'll enjoy using.

Buy the fancy notebook, open it to a double-page spread somewhere in the middle, and start writing down everything you know already about your novel. Draw circles and arrows. Add coloured pens to your shopping list. Have fun.

But. Don't tell yourself you're writing when you're planning. It's a different thing.

There's one danger with plans, and it is that plans can be used for procrastination (I'll get to that later).

Okay, I've said it. Back to the positives.

Plans can also be used to get you started again, keep you on track, remind you where you need to go next.

When you're written out for the day, but you're not quite ready to stop, you can wind down by writing a mini-plan for tomorrow.

[If it's conceivably possible to do so, write – or at least connect with your novel – every day. But don't beat yourself up if you can't. We'll get to this later.]

Planning is a very personal thing. I would like to say: this is how you do it. And give you *The Definitive How-to-Plan Guide*. But I can't. Your plan is how your creative intelligence squares up to the task of starting, or continuing, or finishing, your novel. It's the structure you need to support your writing. And that's up to you.

You have my full permission to charge into writing and make a plan later, or to draw up a detailed plan and stick to it. Either is good, and so is everything in between.

Oh, and one final thing. Nobody has to see your plan. There's no pressure.

Enjoy yourself with those coloured pens.

How Novels Start

We've talked about writing sentences - and not necessarily Opening Sentences - as a way of lifting the curtain. We've talked about planning. Now here's just a brief observation that might be useful.

However enormous the world you're building, or however complex the character you want to depict, chances are your novel will start with a tiny mundane scene in which something apparently ordinary happens. The kid who's going to save the universe glances out of the window. The elderly artist who's locked down at home, er, glances out of the window. And they're both doing the washing up.

Novels start by lifting the curtain. They don't rip it aside. [Except when they do. We come to that in the section *Working with Characters*, which is up ahead.]

I am **not** saying that you have to start writing your novel at the beginning – although a lot of novelists do.

I **am** saying: do **not** be afraid of the beginning.

Your opening scene will be a scene like any other (but probably smaller).

Don't stress over it.

Questions Novelists Don't Ask

When you start writing, don't second-guess yourself.

Don't ask yourself: is this my opening scene?

Don't follow that up with: is this the best opening scene my novel could have?

Should I start again with a better opening scene?

No!

Just write. Keep writing.

You **may not** have just written your opening scene (even if you think you have). But you **absolutely have** written a necessary scene.

To illustrate that by way of an example – you may have started with something like this.

Gerbil raised his hands from the washing-up water and looked out of the window. The gates were open and the drawbridge was down. The King would be arriving soon, and with him the whole Court.

Assuming you keep going, the King arrives, et cetera,

17

and all the plates are clean for the banquet, and Gerbil – that's the nickname they gave him because of his, I don't know, looks – gets bullied by the high-born older boys, and/or gets noticed by the King, and/or pulls a carving knife out of a stone – and you're on your way.

Later, very much later, you may decide that your novel should start with the banquet, so Gerbil's washing-up scene gets dropped, or he's washing up afterwards and watching the King leave, or … I don't know what, but my point is: **you only have a King, and a Court, and a drawbridge and gates, et cetera, because you went ahead with your first impulse to write about Gerbil looking out of the window.**

With that **first** scene, you've done so much already.

Write!

How Novelists Pretend to Start

Back in *How Novels Start*, I gave two examples of tiny mundane opening scenes in which something apparently ordinary happens.

The kid who's going to save the universe glances out of the window. The elderly artist who's locked down at home glances out of the window. They're both doing the washing up.

That kid is daydreaming about piloting his own spaceship one day. That elderly artist is thinking: maybe I could paint a picture of birds in flight. Both are meticulous about how they rinse and dry the spoons, and that meticulous attention to the cutlery is a really clever way of showing us one aspect of who they'll turn out to be.

Ace pilot capable of really precise flying; brilliant artist with a talent for detail.

Shouldn't you be trying to do something like that?

No!

Start writing your novel with a high tolerance for chaos

and contradiction. All those clever touches that will so impress your readers – they'll come to you later; add them later.

You have to live with your characters for a while, and write a lot about them, before you can be certain that you know them well enough to fine-tune their quirky little habits. And tip off readers via their meticulous (or not) washing-up skills.

One day, you might meet readers who assume that the novel you published is exactly the novel you meant to write, all along, and that the opening scene – so clever! – is exactly the opening scene you meant to write – and did write, on Day One.

You'll know better.

But you won't tell, will you?

How to Read the Rest of This Book

This is no time to be reading long stretches of narrative blah-blah about what you're doing.

You need suggestions and ideas and examples.

So from here on I'm using bullet points.

You could use the Contents Page as a checklist of priorities. or you could flick though the whole of this book when you're done writing for the day, or you could check whichever section applies to whatever you're expecting to write next.

I don't want to tell you how to read the rest of this book, actually.

From here on, it's a collection of suggestions, etc., that can be read in any order.

I hope you find a way to read it that makes it useful to you.

- I've made up my own examples because we're not here to be admiring successful authors (and possibly getting discouraged by how good they are). We want to be doing this together, you and I.

• You can't start to write your first novel by following instructions. That exercise with the three sentences – I didn't tell you what the three sentences had to be. You had to make them up for yourself.

✱ You have to start your first novel with your own idea for a novel.

• There's any amount of software available; there are any number of online courses, creative-writing classes, books like this one, books not like this one, fellow authors, helpful friends – to support you once you've started, and it would be just about possible to continue writing and then finish your first novel by following instructions.

But don't do that.

You're not writing your first novel because it's a sensible career option (although it might turn out that way), and nor are you writing it because you want to be the next somebody else.

You're writing your first novel because you have it in you.

Because you want to be you.

Don't follow instructions.

Listen, learn, read, pay attention at the back, take all the support you can get – and then write your own first novel, your own way.

I hope you find the rest of my book useful as you do that. Enough talk.

Have You Started Yet?

- Start writing. Do it now. We've talked about this.

  Plan as much as you like, but also — start writing.

  If you've got an Opening Sentence, great, but you can start writing anywhere.

  Or give yourself a prompt for any old mundane scene that might fit in your novel.

  He woke up, for example, or *She opened her eyes*.

  You can delete it later, but you need to be writing your novel.

- Procrastination – no, I'll get to that later.

- Write it forward.

  He woke up. Myrna was snoring.

  If you've got the first sentence, what matters is the second sentence, and then the third. We've talked about this, too.

The room was dark.

Time spent wondering whether that first sentence should be *He awoke* is wasted.

And who's Myrna anyway?

Writing is also a way of inventing the questions that will take the story forward.

• You can even start with *He stared at the blank screen*, or *She*, because if you're really stuck, it'll be the second or third sentence that gets you started. Once you've got a few details to rub together, you'll find it easier to invent more.

She stared at the blank screen. This was her only time to write. She spent all day working in her dead-end job at ... and—Go!

• Write!

• Write now, edit later. You want three adequate chapters more than you want nineteen over-polished versions of the same opening sentence.

• You can always delete it. Or change it. Later. Not now. **No!**

• Write!

• Go into detail.
He woke up. He got up. He started his day.
All true, but how does he take his coffee?

He woke up. Next detail, please.

This is NOT where you drop in the complete and total biography (I'm coming to that), but what woke him? What's around him?

You and your reader are with him as he wakes up. What do you (all) notice?

Start writing.
Keep writing.
Finish the story.

26

What Happens Next?

- Something has to happen.

Your brilliant (adequate is enough, remember) opening scene will hold the attention for maybe a couple of pages, but after that—move! Change it up. Action.

If you're happily writing a scene and it's turning into a comfort zone, get out of it. That applies throughout the novel.

- Characters take themselves for granted. They don't pause on Page Three to reflect that they were born here, brought up there, traumatised there, married, divorced, blah blah, life story and let's just check what I look like in the mirror ... only getting back to their coffee and croissant on Page Nine.

The more effective your opening, the more totally the info-dump kills it.

Occasional memories maybe, a touch of background, a paragraph or two, but mostly, show your characters being themselves and let your readers work out who they are.

Necessary info tends to fall naturally into place – but I'm coming to that.

• You know more than you think you know about how police investigations, covert operations, et cetera, work. We've all watched television. I'm not saying don't do any research, but don't do it first.

Don't be put off from even starting your crime novel, for example, by the thought that you've never been inside a police station.

• You've never been inside a space station either. But who's going to tell you you're wrong?

• Don't skip the difficult scenes. If you're coming up to a scene that's going to be impossible to write, write it. You'll learn a lot more from the attempt, than you will from cutting straight from the 'before' to the 'after'. You might even succeed.

Sex scenes are the exception—you can cut from 'before' to 'after' without missing anything. We know what they're doing. [Although I remember a first-time novelist who was told/asked by the mainstream publisher who had just accepted her first novel to put in more sex.]

• You're going to have to create characters you don't like. Just saying. They're going to do things you wouldn't do. You have to let them. In fact, you have to make them.

• Strictly speaking, this belongs in the sequel – what do you think of *Beyond Getting Started* for a title? – but I'll say it anyway. There will come a point, maybe ten, twenty pages in, when you need to up your game. You'll recognise it by how it makes you feel.

Your main character has arrived in town (for example), found a flat, found a job, made some friends, kept her secrets, beaten off some enemies, generally made a good start, and, um, yeah, she could go on doing all that for the rest of the novel.

But you're starting to feel a bit – meh.

How shall I put this?

Your main character could keep scrambling happily (-ish) around in the foothills, but she's come here to climb the mountain.

She's broken in her new boots, tried on her oxygen mask (several times) and practised putting up her tent on a vertical slope.

But she hasn't looked up.

The mountain is *there*.

This is the point in the novel at which you give your main character a purpose.

She's set herself up in her new life, but – so what?

Is there a big mountain to climb?

What's the main objective that she'll be working towards over the course of the novel?

You need that purpose too, I suggest. That's what you're feeling.

Guess the novel?

29

If your main character is a detective, give her a murder. If she's a superhero, give her a supervillain. If she's (he's) a lightly fictionalised version of you, give her (him) a [*you tell me*].

If she's a mountaineer give her a mountain.

Yeah, and maybe show her the latest weather forecast as well.

There's a storm front coming in. Snow, fog, hail, lighting, freezing rain, blizzards and that really annoying drizzle that gets right down the back of your neck – all due to arrive simultaneously a week from now (the weather in this novel is atrocious).

If she doesn't get climbing now, there's a risk she'll get caught on the North Face – the one they call *El Muerte*. *El Muerte Muerte*

Oh, and here's the guy who'll be going with her.

! We did tell her, didn't we, that <u>she's not allowed</u> to attempt this on her own?

She does realise that they've put her together with – this guy?

This isn't a rom-com, is it? Surely not?

Bet he wants to go via the South Face – the one they call *El Easy*.

Oh, they're going to argue.

[I can't imagine myself ever using this sudden, spontaneous rom-com complication, but do you see how it gives me a possible direction? Give your mountaineer a companion, or your detective a murder(er), superhero a supervillain, etc., and all of a sudden you know where you **could** take the rest of your novel. See also the short item about setting up an expectation in the next section.]

Top of page 33

How To Write

Say it straight. Don't wrap it up in clever phrases.

The best writing aims to be **transparent**: when you evoke a feeling, the reader feels it. She doesn't think to herself: that's a clever description.

Don't be clever. Your reader is your equal partner in the experience of reading your novel.

Feelings are individual but they are also universal. You *can* imagine how your character feels in that situation. Don't skip the difficult scenes.

Write to somebody. Writing is always one-to-one communication. I'm talking to you, not addressing a lecture-hall packed (I wish) with everybody who'll ever read this. However imaginary your reader might be, write as though you're telling your story to a single reader.

You're not Writing, capital W. This is not some special thing that you have to learn to do. You're telling a story. You're talking one-to-one with each of your readers. Writing doesn't exactly come naturally, but you've got the basics already.

There's a distinction between "showing" (which is thought to be good) and "telling" (which is thought to be not so good). You can use both, but the idea is, "showing" has more dramatic impact.

If you want to get across that your character is startled, *"Eek! Help! Argh!" he said* would be showing it, while *He was startled, so he cried out* would be telling it.

Something like that.

If you don't need the *he said/she said* because it's obvious who's talking, I say: leave it out.

If you do need the *he said/she said*, probably leave it at that. Sometimes, you'll need *he shouted* or *she explained* or possibly even *he said hastily*, but don't drag your reader through every possible variation on *he said*. The conversation doesn't flow (he vouchsafed categorically).

Rhythm. Vary it. At the simplest level—short sentences, long sentences; action, description, dialogue.

"Write like you talk" has always been good advice, and now there are audiobooks. Punctuation is pausing to draw breath.

✱ If you set up an expectation—so that the reader is pretty sure of what's going to happen next—either deliver on it or make some kind of a surprise out of it not happening. The serial killer gets the babysitter in his car—and drives her home.

Once you've set up an expectation, you can deliver the expected or the unexpected, but you can't ignore it.

Verisimilitude. Fine example of a long word that means a simple thing. You want your characters to be living a life that feels real while your reader is reading it.

guess Not sure why, but strangely often this turns out to mean an opening scene in which the main character is hung over, broke, on the run, out of work, not quite over her ex, and about to be evicted. It's raining. Thank [*expletive deleted*] for the sympathetic bartender whose patience hasn't quite run out.

We should mention "suspension of disbelief" here as well.

Nobody in fiction ever trusts the mysterious, morally questionable, definitely untrustworthy but spectacularly good-looking benefactor who turns up unexpectedly just after the last possible moment and offers a way out. He's always offering a job that will be risky, that she doesn't want but will have to take.

Sorry. Many of those books are very readable. And if I'm going to get away with saying all that about a sub-genre of fantasy/private-eye fiction that I enjoy reading (but don't tell anybody), I should also acknowledge that familiar elements in a plot (in the sense: you feel that you've read them before) can contribute to a comfortable read.

33

The hero *always* turns down the Hero's Journey first time it's offered. We know this.

Talking about familiar elements – there are archetypes in storytelling. Archetypal situations and archetypal characters. Feel free to look them up, but don't panic. What matters is that you write your story. There are **NO** archetypes that you have to include in your novel. They are optional.

They can be useful, though, for plotting (see also the section conveniently headed *Plotting* later), and they're a large part of the reason why certain elements – I really mean characters, but situations as well – may seem familiar.

That old guy in the pointed hat telling you what to do with the ring you've found, and this other desert-dwelling guy suggesting you go with him to the space-port, and let's not forget the old buffer in tweeds telling you that garlic around the windows will keep out vampires – there's a reason why they turn up early on.

Yes, it is simply that the Hero needs a way to go and some know-how.

But the Hero has always needed such support, in all the stories ever told that begin with a Hero reluctantly packing bags (Heroes are always reluctant to set off), so the Sage is always on-hand to contribute.

There'll be a Sidekick along in a moment, just you wait, and what do you think of this sneaky-looking person who's so keen to know all your secrets?

We've grown up with archetypes. In a good way, they're in our heads. It would be hard to write a novel without a few of them just naturally turning up.

Find out about them, consciously use them if you want to, but beyond that, just write. They'll come if you need them.

If a sentence, or a paragraph, just won't work, stop. Take a breath. Start again. But this time, start with the words "What I'm trying to say here is..."

If the words won't come at all, take a hike and/or a shower. Leave behind every possible writing implement. Put everything out of reach.

Work the shampoo into a really good lather.

Make it totally 100% top-of-the-mountain/suds-in-your-eyes impossible to write anything down.

Then the words will come.

The greatest skill of all is to write down *exactly* the perfect sentence that has just come into your head. Don't edit. Don't improve. Don't even *think* until it's safely written down.

Keep your readers wanting to know more. That's obvious. More importantly, as you write, keep yourself at least partially in the dark.

Don't plan so rigidly that you can't surprise yourself.

Reading needs to engage the reader's imagination.

Writing needs to engage the writer's imagination.

More on this in *How Writing Works* later.

There is no substitute for wanting to know what happens next.

Ideas come while you're writing. Sometimes, while you're planning, but always, while you're writing. Is this you?

He sat at the table with his laptop open in front of him. There was noise in the cafe but he'd tuned it out. All that mattered was the screen and the empty document.

'Chapter 1,' he typed, then deleted it and typed 'Chapter One' instead.

Well done, you've started. You've already got a noisy cafe. But let's get out of this comfort zone. Let's see, how can we do this? Bring in somebody else?

"What are you writing?" she asked as she put down his latte. Her turn to buy; she'd insisted.

"A massive fantasy epic involving a guy who writes a book that comes true around him," he said.

"Can I read what you've written so far?"

"Er, I haven't really started today."

He deleted 'One' and typed 'Nine' instead.

He wasn't going to tell her he hadn't started at all.

I kind of almost want to write that. Why was it her turn to buy? I thought she was the barista bringing over his coffee until I wrote that sentence.

I can keep writing and find out why it was her turn, or I can invent a reason and put it in a plan. I know which I'd prefer to do.

He drinks *latte*? I had him pegged as an espresso person.

You know what I think about plans by now. Planning is great, but it isn't writing. No plan needs to survive first contact with the keyboard. If your writing is taking you off somewhere else, let it. You can rewrite the plan later but you'll never get those spontaneous ideas back if you block them now.

"Find it in the writing of your plan" is a thing people say. It doesn't mean the same as: make a plan. Sometimes, the simplest way to add a scene to your plan ... is to write the scene. Sometimes, a snatch of dialogue just occurs to you. Add it to the plan. When planning turns into writing ... go with writing.

Any novel has its own way of being written. You work out how to do it while you're doing it.

If you're thinking that the time has come to close this book and get on with it – follow your instinct. Your novel needs what it needs. If it's calling you, it's coming alive.

There's no "should" in writing. Is it readable? Does it say what you want it to say? Nothing else matters.

The words that matter are the words that the reader will see. If you're not writing those, you're not writing. You can do the planning and all the rest of it, and that's okay, but—don't count it as writing.

[This is just a personal gripe. If your hero is immortal (for example), it is not a viable plot twist to have her discover early on that she's not immortal any more. If your readers are looking forward to reading about a main character who can fly (for another example), don't start with her discovering that she can't fly any more.]

Give your readers a break occasionally. You decide when a new chapter is needed, and how long it has to be. There's no rule.

Give your chapters cliff-hanger endings. Or don't.

Like everything else, that's up to you.

Yes, of course you can use novel-writing software. As much as you like. If you find a program that gives you the initial idea and gets you started, let me know.

Until you know how the book ends (because you've written a provisional ending), you can't usefully obsess over getting the beginning right. Keep going.

Trust your book to end. You may (or may not) see how it's going to end early on. You may (or may not) have been inspired to write the ending shortly after you wrote the beginning. Don't worry if not. Just write. Do that, and you'll get there.

Working with Characters

• Characters are important. There are novels that consist of nothing more than one character thinking, and there are novels in which nobody does any thinking at all – they leap out of aeroplanes, jump out of trucks, shoot each other, smoulder with lust at each other and, um, get very close together – all without any detectable brain-work.

But I can't think of a single novel in which there are no characters at all.[*]

The good news – spoiler for this section – is that characters come naturally. We are all characters in our own lives. Each of us has direct lived experience of how one character operates, and a lot of observational evidence as to how a wide range of other characters operate.

I could just say: characters are people and we know how people work.[**]

[**] Robots, AIs, aliens, ghosts and animals all count as characters.

[*] If you can, let me know. But before you do, read the novel and ask yourself: "Who's speaking?" See also How to Write-Cute later.

But no. Let's work through this. There are some practical suggestions ahead, and some examples, and a big think-through about how to introduce and develop characters, and keep them interesting.

Here goes.

• Work with characters from the inside: however many medals your character may have on her chest, she was a baby once and is a human being now. [Unless she's a cardboard cut-out – that's coming up.]

Write three sentences with a *He* or a *She* in them, or a gender-neutral pronoun, and you create a character. That is one approach to starting a working relationship with a character. Novels often start with tiny mundane scenes in which your character(s) can be shown performing ordinary tasks in, well, characteristic ways (see *How Novels Start* earlier but also *How Novelists Pretend to Start*). They grow as characters as you write and we read them.

• What if you don't want to do it that way? What if you want to start your novel by jumping straight into your action-packed galactic clash of civilisations?

What if you want to do that with heavily armed spaceships rather than boring old characters?

Let's try it.

Uh, no, wait.

I think I am going to start with a rank and a name. Very senior rank, to get across that this is a high-level start.

A character, you might think, but not really; just rank and name.

It's an effective way – and a lot of novelists use it – of putting the reader *right there* without having to say too much of anything about the – well, character – behind the rank and the name and the uniform and the medals and the good looks and the crazy skills, etc., etc., and the simple function in the story.

You could go with *Vast battle-cruisers moved through the emptiness of space, bristling with weapons. Some were sleek and silver, as beautiful as they were lethal, and others were black lumps, shapeless as coal* – or something like that.

But even then, sooner or later, I suggest that you would need to bring in somebody to give an order or press a button or pull a trigger.

[Yes, in my galactic clash of civilisations, we do have both buttons and triggers. Where there are triggers, sooner or later you're going to need a finger tightening on a trigger.]

So let's get the kind-of-necessary but minimal rank-and-name involvement in my opening scene right up front and out of the way so that we can jump straight into the battle.

Here goes.

Admiral of the Fleet Dwight J Carpenter stood on the bridge of his flagship, the Star-Carrier Freehold Endeavour, *and stared at the alien battle-fleet on the view-screen in front of him.*

So many ships. So much hostility.

And yet he knew that this was a day Earth could win. They'd discussed tactics; they'd identified and analysed the aliens' weaknesses. And now he had the aliens exactly where he wanted them.

He spoke, knowing without having to look that his Executive Officer, Commander Lucia Bradley, was standing behind him to the left. "We're ready to engage?"

"Of course, Boss."

She called him Boss at times of tension, and he allowed it.

"Fire," he said, and the white-out on the viewscreen told him that his order had broadcast simultaneously across the fleet, to Weapons Officers with their fingers already on their consoles.

That was okay, wasn't it? Hardly a page in, and they're already shooting at each other.

Yes, I want to know what happens next.

Does Earth win?

Is there a second alien fleet hiding behind a planet nearby?

From that beginning, I would guess that you're going to show me the battle next, and then maybe Chapter Two is going to start with some background. I'm even set up to want to know more.

When did the aliens first appear?

How's the war going?

Uh, yeah. I did write it, didn't I? Thank you for the reminder.

That's what I would do. Knowing the deadening effect of the info-dump (see under *What Happens Next?* earlier), I would try to fit the necessary information (see also *The Urge to Explain* later) into the story in a way that didn't block the flow. I'd mix in lots of battle tactics and lots of explosions.

What I would **not** do, not even be **tempted** to do, is drop in a slab of background information on Admiral Carpenter, nor on Commander Bradley.

After all, they are essentially just character-sized **cardboard cut-outs** with the simple function of getting the guns to fire.

Rank and name. Hardly characters at all.

And info-dumps are a no-no anyway. We know that.

Right?

Look, I've done what you asked me to do. You've got your battle scene.

But.

Wait a minute.

Are those two just going to disappear, now that they've served their purpose?

That was the idea, I know.

And they could, perfectly easily, disappear.

Just don't mention them again and they're gone.

But.

Let's just think about this for a second.

As I wrote them into my big opening scene, I couldn't help but imagine them. Everything between *exactly where he wanted them* and *"Fire," he said* was me just – writing them as they came into my head.

I **could** file it away for future reference that Carpenter has the aliens where he wants them – he's confident – but Bradley calls him "Boss" when she's nervous – she's not confident – and he allows it – because, I don't know, he likes her?

That **could** be a start to their mini-story within the big story. Occasional moments of human interest for when the explosions get too loud. [We've talked about rhythm, haven't we?]

I **could** just move my spaceships around the galaxy with the occasional cardboard cut-out shouting "Fire!"

And occasionally "Argh!"

No problem with that.

But Carpenter and Bradley are available to participate in the story if I decide that I need them.

And all I did was write them.

My action-packed galactic clash of civilisations has started.

Among the optional accessories available for me to pick up as I write it are – two characters.

A man who is confidently steering Earth's fleet into a head-on battle with the aliens, and a woman who is a lot less confident than he is.

On Page One of what is planned to be a very long novel.

What could possibly go wrong?

I'm glad I wrote them in.

They're giving me ideas.

• Characters are unavoidable. They are present from whenever you first mention them, and whatever you say about them is the beginning of who they are.

To work with characters over novel-time, bring them

back in again as necessary and expand on what we know about them as necessary. Characters form most effectively by the steady accretion of detail. Like stalagmites and stalactites.

You've probably guessed by now that Carpenter only got through the Academy because his father had political connections.

Bradley graduated top in her year. Lots of honours.

She only scraped into the Academy on a scholarship, but once she was in, she was top in everything.

That's enough about them for now. Anything else you need to know – I'll invent it when you need to know it.

I've made this sound like a mechanistic process. Rank and name to define function; sprinkle on a few details; add more details as required.

But really what's going on when we work with characters is – we're getting to know them.

I'm now 800-ish words on from writing the words *Admiral of the Fleet Dwight J Carpenter* for the first (and only?) time, and I kind of know him. He exists for me. As the novel goes on, if I need him again, I'll find out more about him.

This is closer to curiosity than planning, and perhaps not a million miles from a free-association game.

Carpenter is confident, so let's say he's over-confident, so let's say something goes wrong with his strategy, which could mean he's not as bright as he thinks he is, which could tell us something about his education…

As for Bradley – okay, here's some invention based on what's been said already.

He over-ruled her on strategy, after she protested vehemently that they were being drawn into a trap. Now she's doing her duty by standing behind him, but she's not going to let him lose the fleet...

...so she's spoken privately to her network of contacts across the other ships – and her warnings are the only reason any of them are going to survive what's about to happen.

No, I don't know what's about to happen.

Yet.

I'll just have to trust myself to think of something.

[That's the way to do it. Write "what's about to happen" even if you don't know what's about to happen. Trust yourself.]

If you're new to working with characters, I'd say: let them reveal themselves to you on the page.

Let the words you're writing gradually illuminate them, and then ease them out from wherever they are in your imagination.

• You may want to start by ripping the curtain aside to show a big, dramatic scene.

I might talk about writing three sentences and arriving at a small scene.

We're both right.

But Carpenter and Bradley. They're there. I can see them.

You can too, can't you?

• What makes characters "real" is that they have character

(duh). There's depth as well as detail. They live more-than-one-dimensional lives and they contrast with each other.

Carpenter displays photographs in his private quarters – photographs of him meeting important people, shaking hands with presidents, getting medals, et cetera. Bradley has a drawer-full of family photos and other mementos including – quirky details are good – an antique Iron Maiden poster folded up and tucked into the back of her journal.

If you want to know why she has that poster – I'll have to invent a reason. That just came to me, so I put it in.

Give me a moment...

Characters don't have to be complex, fallible, authentic human beings for us to accept them as characters – and care enough about their fate to keep reading – but it helps.

They can be sketched in lightly or obviously – those two large men with shaved heads, broken noses, muscles bulging under their jackets probably haven't come about the babysitting job. They can be clichés, frankly.

You can use your characters as cardboard cut-outs who give orders and then disappear.

You can drop in a few more-or-less random but thought-provoking details about your characters – to make you think about who they are, as much as to interest your reader – or you can engage with your characters fully and even tell the story in their voices.

You can write a totally character-driven novel.

You can write a short novel about the mutated-virus outbreaks of the mid-2020s in which the main character is "obviously" you – or isn't, but all your friends tell you it is.

It's up to you.

• Speaking of more-or-less random but thought-provoking details. That Iron Maiden poster. I've got it now. There was a partner. They planned a life together. She was – they were – blissfully happy. Now that he's lost, she bitterly regrets mocking his enthusiasm for the history of loud music (as she put it). She keeps the poster to remember him by (and to beat herself up by).

I say "lost," not "dead".

He was on a scouting mission deep into alien space. Transmissions from his ship ceased. All contact was lost. That was years ago. He's missing, presumed dead.

It is very, **very** unlikely, almost impossible in fact, million-to-one chance, totally inconceivable almost, that he could be alive somewhere, surviving in the wreckage of his ship, life-support holding up for now, bodging together a comms unit that he won't be able to use because – unless they're beaten back to about as far as they will be beaten back at around three-quarters of the way through the novel – the aliens will pick up the signal and come for him.

Totally unlikely.

Only a reader could hope for such an outcome.

But **if** – I'm saying if, big **if** – there is a reader-pleasing tearful reunion somewhere in the happy ending phase, and let's say that by then Bradley is the main character, she will be going on and on about how he can play his music as loud as he likes, and he won't know what she's talking about (he's discovered alien music and forgotten heavy metal).

They'll probably adopt the alien baby he found abandoned in the – um, somewhere – and cared for while he was lost. The alien baby will turn out to be the child of – working on it – and will grow up to be – I think I need to stop this now. I'm writing *this* book.

Characters stay in character. The admiral isn't going to turn into a strategic and tactical genius any time soon, while Bradley – from what we've said about her so far – probably won't be making too many mistakes between now and the end of the war. But she does have feelings, doesn't she? An inner life.

Be aware of continuity, as well. If any two of your characters have a conversation in Chapter Three, they will remember it when they talk again in Chapter Four. They may pick up where they left off (but if you can resist it, don't add the explanation *They picked up where they left off*).

Real people notice what goes on around them, react to it, and it stays with them through their day. If your characters experience (express) continuity, even in small ways, it can help to bind your novel together as a whole. [I'm not saying that characters can't grow and change over the course of your novel; just that they're the same character underneath.]

Surely somebody in Chapter Five remembers the thunderstorm in Chapter Four? They're all acting as though they're **not** soaking wet. Oops.

We know so much about them already!

Sometimes, characters take over. You'll know what that means when it happens. It's good. Go with it. If a minor character suddenly becomes a major character, or takes over the plot, for example, that means the whole of your brain is working on this story, and not just the conscious part you think you're using.

• Even main characters don't always operate single-handed. Particularly for a series, but also for a stand-alone novel, you may find that your main character works best if supported by a (probably small) number of recurring minor characters.

There might be, for example, the best friend, the boyfriend, the girlfriend, the bartender, the police sergeant, the informant, the mechanic, the infallible assassin (and lifelong friend) who frightens off baddies, the barista, the neighbour, the uncle or the supernatural being, among others who might just turn up in your story to offer support and/or advice and/or weapons when needed.

Your main character might visit such a minor character in that minor character's regular (characteristic) location, or the minor character might come out to join the battle (decisively) at the crucial moment.

Such characters may not want to take over, but they're good to have around. Readers tend to like them. Give them their scene(s), don't over-use them, and keep them consistent.

• Characters often have a symbiotic relationship with their home locations. You can't take the character out of –

wherever it might be – without losing quite a lot of regular places to visit and minor characters who are familiar to the reader – the coffee shop containing the barista, the bar containing the bartender, and so on, as above.

If you get successful with a series, you might find it tax-deductible to set Book Ten in an exotic location overseas where you've always wanted to go on holiday. Fine, but as your main character leaves her hotel, or breaks out of local-police custody, etc., don't be surprised if your writing takes you to a bar, say, where the bartender is a complete stranger ... with some familiar characteristics.

It may not be that direct and obvious, but if you take your main character somewhere new, be prepared for your writing to turn that location into a home from home.

The scariest part of all of this, I suspect, is somewhere between lack of confidence and losing control. Let go. Trust your imagination to know who it needs in your novel as well as where it's all going – which translates as "make it up as you go along" but with added self-confidence – and if your characters start misbehaving in ways that absolutely do not fit with The Plan, don't try to wrench them back into the cosy tea party of a narrative that you were constructing.

Let them break out of the playpen.

who said that?

- Dialogue is two people each waiting for the other to shut up so they can say their next thing. Or it's two people not listening to each other. It's also a visible sign of the ongoing relationship they have with each other, if any.

Mother talks to (adult) son is different from (adult) woman talks to male friend.

Either of those pairings, by the way, would give you any number of possible plot-driving questions. Woman/male friend: does one of them want more? Did they ever, and would they again? Go on—write them and find out.

I wonder if the mother is secretly convinced her son's guilty (suddenly we are writing a crime novel)—and I wonder if she's right about that. Get writing.

If the woman and her male friend, or the mother and her son, turn out to have completely different relationships from what you were expecting/planning when you started to write them, keep going—all complications are welcome while you're putting together a plot. You can delete (some of) them later.

• Another approach to dialogue is to track what's going through each character's mind. What they say is as much a by-product of that as a response to whatever the other character is saying. The mother wants everybody else in the room to think well of her son (or not).

The Urge to Explain

• Keep the story moving. Don't look back. That explanation you think you need to go back and put in? That slab of back story? Chances are, you don't. Let the reader figure it out. [Much, much later, when you're doing the final edit, you can agonise over whether to explain more. Chances are you'll still decide to trust the reader.]

• Genuinely necessary background information tends to fall naturally into place.

(Adult) woman watched her male friend talking to the detectives.

She hadn't wanted to end their relationship, but after eight years, she'd felt that she still didn't really know him.

"What do they think happened?" she asked him, as he came back and sat down next to her on the sofa.

She thought of moving to the armchair.

Didn't really trust him, either.

Bit clunky, but she had to be thinking something as she watched him. [And maybe we can work with him wanting to get closer to her (again) and her not trusting him. He's either trustworthy or he isn't...]

- Reading is active. It's working it out. It isn't passively being told.

How Writing Works

- Your task is to get (and keep) the reader's imagination working. Not to do all the work yourself.

He woke up. Myrna was snoring. The room was dark. 04:58. No point in trying to get back to sleep now. He stood at the window looking down at his car in the deserted car park and remembering...

Can you see them? What about the room? That's a double bed, right?

Where's the clock?

Aha! I thought you'd put it there.

I'm happy to work with your imagination on the interior decoration as well as everything else. If the author spells everything out, what's left for the reader to do?

- If I tell you that I'm writing this in a coffee shop on a street corner, chances are that your imagination will give you a provisional picture of a coffee shop on a street corner.

Your picture will adapt to whatever details I may provide

– because I want to bring this location into line with the needs of my story.

There may be another table, with people at that table who get involved in my story, or for example the suspect may be sitting over there in the corner reading a newspaper.

I do need to give you the details that my story needs. But **only** those details (and maybe a few more for atmosphere – see below).

What I do **not** need to do is supply so much detail that I overwrite your picture of a coffee shop with the one in my head. That would be impossible anyway.

Happy to be using your coffee shop while I write my book. Thank you. Good coffee!

• You may wake up in the middle of the night and decide that your novel needs an atmosphere. By which I mean, you may want to set an overall mood. You may decide that there needs to be a "feel" to this novel that is (a) distinctive and (b) appropriate to the story.

If so, don't worry about it but do be aware of it. An atmosphere doesn't just happen, not exactly, but if you've got a feel for the world you're creating – if you're feeling the atmosphere every time you write – that atmosphere will come across in the writing.

Trust me on this.

Everything in a novel contributes to the atmosphere – everything from the details you pick out in the coffee shops, to whether or not the characters stop and watch the sunsets, to the amount of time they spend thinking about what's going on, to their moods, to what they wear, to the length of the sentences, to the length of the descriptive passages, to the constant rain, to the trees in the forest and whether they blow in the wind or cast long dark shadows.

The atmosphere of your novel is somewhere between the theme tune and the set design. It is, by definition, a mood thing, infused into your novel as you write it.

Let's go back to that coffee shop I mentioned earlier. I've told you about that lovely coffee aroma, haven't I? And the sunlight glancing off the silver coffee machine and Angie's easy laughter across the counter as she flirts with a regular customer? And the breeze through the big open windows, and the tiny white sails far out on the bay?

Did I also tell you about the musty old coffee shop with the damp-stained walls painted in the colour of blood and the heavy curtains like shrouds, where the failing twilight barely penetrates the grime on the windows? That portrait – over there, that dark old oil painting in the heavy gilt frame. I could swear he's looking at me.

This carpet is sticky!

As you write, if you always know that the bay is there, with the white sails, you'll probably make the sun bright in that novel and all the coffee machines silver. Angie will work her way into the story somehow.

But if the failing twilight never penetrates the grime on the windows, and the Count never takes his eyes off you – well, I wouldn't drink the coffee in that novel. But I would avoid the dark corners. Of which there would be many.

Atmosphere is the choices you make and the words you use and how you feel about what's happening on the page. It's the quality of the light and the dark. It's what your characters glimpse out of the car window as they drive through the forest.

If you want an atmosphere – feel it.

- *"Do you remember?" he said.*

  She looked up at him.

  "Of course I remember," she said, and then again, softly, "Of course I remember."

  She took his hand and they stood together at the end of the jetty and watched as the sun went down over the water.

I've no idea what that's about, but I wanted to give another example where the words on the page are just the starting point for imagining the scene.

Can you see them? Do you have a sense of their relationship? How tall is she? Anything else you want to know? I hope so.

- Incidentally, in that example of the couple on the jetty, I'm torn between *and watched* and *to watch*. This is a fine example of the kind of question that should be left until a lot more writing has happened.

  What do they remember? Are they a couple?

  This was their custom. To watch the sunset on their last evening together and then drive back separately from the boat house to the city.

  "Of course I remember," she said once again, alone in her car, watching the tail lights of his car recede into the distance.

  The question had stuck with her: did he really think she could

60

ever forget that magical evening when they'd found a copy of William Essex's **God — The Interview and other stories** *in their favourite bookstore?*

This book contains product placement. Sorry. Couldn't resist.

• Here comes another question - *watching / as she watched the tail lights*—argh!

• Writing is such an effective way of expressing what you don't write.

That couple on the jetty. What do they feel about each other?

Don't think I wrote that – but it's there.

• Writing is such an effective way of finding what you haven't written yet.

That couple on the jetty. I don't know where they live – yet – but as they drive back homeward, I can feel the whole city opening up before me.

What if they *do* live together?

Driving back from the boat house in separate cars ... why?

Stop! I'm writing *this* book.

Names. They have a shape on the page.
Jonny can't work with Jenny,
and if Marmaduke owns Marmalade,
which one catches the mice?

Avoid confusion.

Facts in Fiction

• Write what you know, but don't be afraid to invent your knowledge. In your book, the spaceships work the way you say they work. In your book, you get to decide whether the vampires can go out in daylight. As I said before, who's going to tell you you're wrong?

• Some readers do have strong views on whether vampires can go out in daylight. Some will tell you very firmly that (for example) zombies can't run fast. You may like to bring in an authority figure early on to explain what's myth and what's real in your novel.

There is a discussion about archetypes in the section *How to Write* earlier. Readers who would criticise you for your sunbathing vampires and sprinting zombies will generally accept the arbitration of your fictional Sage on such disputes.

You still decide, but let the Professor speak your decision.

- There are some things you can't know that (some of) your readers will know only too well. Best example (but not the only example) — the intimate workings of the other kind of human body — male or female, whichever you're not.

You can write from the opposite perspective, and will probably have to sooner or later, but my advice would be, don't go *there*.

- If you get an important detail wrong — embarrassingly wrong, let's say — such a mistake can break the imaginative bond between you and your reader. And that's not cool.

- Research may not be necessary at the outset, but if your characters are going to drive interesting cars, fire unusual guns, use specialist tools, visit real places, et cetera, find out as much as you can about those tools, etc., probably offline as well as online.

Performance cars handle more easily online, for example, than they do on the road.

There are always tricky little details, and there's (almost) always somebody with a large social-media following who's indignant that you got those details wrong.

The ignition on that car doesn't work that way, actually; that gun's magazine has this capacity, actually; you couldn't lift one of those; actually, let alone operate it one-handed, actually. And so on. Actually.

When acknowledging the people who helped you, always say that any remaining mistakes are yours not theirs.

Oh, and of course you can also say that you deliberately,

not mistakenly, adjusted reality to fit with the needs of your story – actually.

• Don't include all your research just because you've done it. There are novels in which it might be appropriate to describe (for example) a journey in detail, but there are others in which the main character knows the journey so well that her describing it would be unreal.

Your research just saves you from niggling mistakes. If you have an English character driving back to London (England) from the West Country, for example, you don't need to explain any more about the route than the main choice – M4 or A303.

But if your character takes the A303, will she see Stonehenge on the **left** or the right of the road? You can bring that in, because your character will look across at the stones.

If in doubt – thick fog has its uses in fiction.

If the only reason you're doing your research is that you've made your character an expert in something – bear in mind that experts only use their expert-talk when they're doing their job.

Overall, authenticity's great, but don't get hung up on it. The world you build has to be real enough for the book you're writing and real enough for your readers to accept.

If they're liking the characters and the story, they'll go along with the way your world works. And probably forgive minor mistakes.

More Product Placement...

- ...and an example completed.

He woke up. Myrna was snoring. The room was dark. 04:58. No point in trying to get back to sleep now. He stood at the window looking down at his car in the deserted car park and remembering his conversation with William Essex yesterday.

*"You're the author of **Escape Mutation—A Journal of the Plague Years**, aren't you?" he had said.*

*"Yes, and **Ten Steps to a Bedtime Story**. Various other books," Essex had replied. "**Can I Quote You on That?** about handling the media." The lecture hall had been empty—hardly anybody had turned up for his lecture on what he knew about writing—but Essex had seemed more amused than disappointed.*

"What are you working on now?"

*"I'm in the middle of a book that I want to call **Write Now—The First-Novelist's Guide to Getting Started.**"*

"Isn't that the whole book in two words?"

Essex had just looked at him.

"I think it's a great title." ?he said ~~lastity~~?

Writers could be so touchy.

*"Maybe I'll cut the **Write Now** bit," Essex had said, and then, "So you'll be staying in a room overlooking the car park on the upper floor of the Travelodge at Reading Westbound Services on the M4 motorway?"*

"Yes. That's the room that my imagination is showing me, at least. It may change when somebody reads this. I'll have Myrna with me, of course."

"Oh, she'll love it."

"I know she will."

A grunting, wheezing, not-quite-barking sound from the far side of the bed told him that Myrna had woken up. He whirled round. "Good dog," he said, as the enormous boarhound stepped down heavily onto the carpet. "Shall we go walkies before breakfast?"

Descriptions and Distractions

- Adjectives are not what they say they are. To say that an experience is "horrible", for example, is not to have your reader feel the horror. To say that a character is "beautiful" is not to convey that character's appearance. You can use adjectives, but understand what they *don't* do.

I'm not sure about adverbs. She says "softly". She says "angrily". Et cetera. Hmm. If "softly" or "angrily" isn't obvious from the context—if your reader won't already know how her voice sounds, just adding the adverb may not be the most effective way to get the emotion across. If the emotion is already obvious—you don't need the adverb anyway. Although sometimes, "softly" (for example) can be a beat in the rhythm of the sentence.

- If your metaphors and similes are too glaringly clever, they'll distract from what you're trying to describe. They're useful tools, but if they stand out from the text around them like a rose-tinted iceberg would stand out from a flat-calm silver sea beneath an endless blue sky dotted with tiny birds like raisins in a cake mix, they might distract from - what was I saying?

People say "kill your darlings". What they usually mean is: if you love, love, love a clever phrase, don't force it in where it'll mess up the flow. *Like adding a searchlight to your party lights.* May I dump that one here?

Plotting

- There is a stage in the writing of a novel at which you have to stop writing and work out what's going on. This is plotting and it tends to arrive quite late in the writing. It tends to follow successive hasty revisions of the original plan due to the spontaneous irruption of new ideas while you've been typing/scribbling away.

Plotting is what you do when you realise that you just can't go on. [Yes, you can still have ideas while you're plotting.]

You finish a draft, and everything is in a muddle. Or you can't finish a draft because everything is in a muddle. You've got scenes that are in the wrong order, events that should happen earlier or later, effects without causes, short-cut tricks that got you from one scene to the next – that you knew you'd have to come back and fix.

There may be whole sub-plots that could be intercut with other sub-plots, to introduce suspense, and characters who died in Chapter Three riding in on horseback in Chapter Four. Or simply: characters know things they haven't been told; they're discussing events that haven't happened yet; they've been married ten years but they've only just met.

Your hero escapes from the island but there's no scene in which he is kidnapped and taken to the island – because you thought of the island later in the writing than the going-there could have happened (I think that makes sense as a summary of something that doesn't?).

On another occasion, your hero walks into a room in which he's already present, or out of a room that's empty.

Several of the characters change their own names over the course of the novel, without noticing.

You can use software for plotting, but there may be a case for making the process three-dimensional. I've heard it described as "going to the cards" by a novelist who writes every scene onto an index card and then shuffles all the cards around on a table, working them into a satisfactory order. Pink cards for romantic scenes, green for description, yellow for action or dialogue, apparently – to get the overall rhythm right.

I've watched another friend spread a print-out of her novel – A4 pages, single-spaced, lots of them – on her floor.

Plotting gives you a readable rhythm – fast scene, slow scene, however you do it – and of course a workable timeline. Also, knowing that eventually there will be a time of reckoning – sorry, I meant plotting – enables you to write freely.

You can write anything if you know that later, you'll be able to delete it.

You should see some of my early – never mind.
And actually you can't. I've deleted them.

Opening scene. You might lift it
from somewhere else in the novel
and put it at the start.

How to Write-Cute

- ## Who's writing this?

    If you're happily telling your story by now, finding the words, writing your novel, not worrying about a thing, don't read this section.

    But - okay - it might be interesting.

    You could write as "I" or you could write as "he, she, they" - you could be a first-person narrator, or a third-person narrator.

    This only matters if you want it to matter, but there are story-telling meta-opportunities (keep reading) to consider.

    Here's what usually happens.

    With a first-person narrator, "I" am part of the story, or I was. It happened to me (or is happening to me).

    With a third-person narrator, "he" and "she" are having their story told for them by the voice of the narrator.

    Okay so far.

    But here's where we get to storytelling-cute.

    What if "I" am deluding myself - and/or you?

What if "I" am unreliable and it didn't happen that way at all? I'm telling the story but I'm actually lying.

What if "his/her" narrator is writing a self-serving report on your characters, because that narrator is their therapist, for example, and the reader doesn't realise that until later in the novel?

Let's not go too deeply into this right now, but - even the voice telling your story can be part of your story.

• In case this needs saying – throughout this book I use he/him and she/her characters in my examples. There is nothing to stop you using gender-neutral pronouns or not revealing gender at all. Same with ethnicity, of course.

And by the way, characters take their own gender and ethnicity for granted along with everything else about themselves. They don't glance in the mirror and say "I'm a man!" If you get to know them, and you write them as they are, chances are you can trust your readers to pick up what needs to be picked up.

There are successful novels in which the name of the main character – the "I" – is never revealed. Love that.

• You need to keep the *deus* in the machine.

If a character is going to need a gun later, you need to show that character picking up a gun earlier. This applies to life as well as fiction. If I'm going to need my phone later, I'd better pick it up now.

A *deus ex machina* is a "god from the machine" where the machine is a crane and the god is lowered into the action of an ancient Greek or Roman drama to decide the outcome. Thanks to merriam-webster.com.

We don't do drama that way any more. But the term survives. It's still used to describe something that is introduced from outside (lowered in) to resolve an issue in the plot, but these days, it's considered cheating and tends to annoy readers.

There is a worthwhile game to be played here, though. If you can disguise/conceal the picking-up of the gun (let's assume it's a gun), you can build up tension and then deliver a satisfying pay-off.

Your character's up the creek without a gun, needs a gun, can't escape without a gun, everything's going horribly wrong without a gun, but at the last moment – your character produces a gun!

And legitimately, too. Your character has to explain, of course, briefly, that when he said earlier, "I picked something else off the shelf as well," he was referring to the gun. Ideally, you will have mentioned already by then, just in passing, perhaps while describing his living space, that your character keeps his guns on the shelf.

Get it right, and you will have a happily surprised reader.

But if your principal villain is struck by a random thunderbolt just as he is about to shoot the hero – nah. Not reading this.

• The 0th draft, zeroth draft, draft zero. This is a popular idea.

You start writing your book and you write. You keep

writing. You don't look back, or edit at all. You just write. Every day. Until you reach the end and then you stop.

Leave it for a bit. Look at it.

What you have in front of you is a little bit (or a lot) of what works and a lot (or a little bit) of what doesn't.

Out of the wreckage that is your completed draft zero, you can salvage maybe one or two fragments (perhaps a lot more than that) plus a clearer idea of what you will put into your first draft and what you won't.

Draft zero gets you deep into novel-writing territory without any nagging sense that every paragraph has to be the best possible way of saying what it says.

• There's also FINMAD, which is a similar idea. As you write your draft zero, Forget Inspiration, Never Miss A Day. Just keep writing. [It's actually BINMAD, but I'm squeamish about certain B-words.]

Editing's Inevitable

• Don't edit anything you've written until you've got some distance from it. You'll know you've got some distance from it when you can read it without immediately thinking that it's brilliant/terrible.

• When you're editing a scene you've written, you'll almost certainly find that deleting words, phrases and even sentences is more effective than adding more words, phrases and even sentences.

• When you edit, you may find that deleting is more effective than adding.

• Odd thing, but where you've over-dramatised an action-word—*He spun round* rather than *He turned round*, for example—you may find that the action is implicit in the

He woke up ~~woke up~~ ~~woke~~ woke up

context. Not every time, but often enough. Always consider deleting the stage direction rather than just changing it (or leaving it if you literally meant that he "spun" round).

• Don't get hung up on grammar or anything else. But do use spellcheck and any other tools. Do be interested in all that. It's better to know the rules and decide to ignore them, than to make mistakes out of ignorance. Also listen out for day-to-day usage. It changes over time and some of the changes stick. Not so long ago, a "big ask" would have been a lot to ask.

• Really don't panic if you don't know what a gerund is. Or a fronted adverbial. Look them up, because you want to develop a habit of being interested in everything (and to improve your writing skills, obviously), but feel free to forget them again afterwards.

• What matters is being able to use words, not to talk about how you use them. Unless you want to, of course.

• Don't get hung up on the not-quite-right bits of your novel either. Edit for flow by reading on through. You can always come back. Sleep on it. Let your brain process.

Awake at 3am?

- Copyright. Nobody's going to steal your work while you're an unknown. Opinions differ as to how bothered you should get about the possibility of miscreants publishing pirated copies of your work when you're famous.

There's also plagiarism, as below. Annoying to be the original author of a paragraph that helps somebody else get famous.

Back in pre-digital times, authors would post copies of their work to themselves, in envelopes addressed so that the date-stamp would go over the seal. Tricks like that to prove that they had the words before anybody else did. A pre-digital version of emailing it to yourself. Or putting it up in the cloud. Just saying.

When you write something, you establish copyright in that form of words. When you write a novel, you own the copyright in that novel. Your copyright also covers the distinctive component parts of your novel: anybody can write a maverick detective with a drink problem, but they can't write **your** maverick detective with a drink problem.

I am **not** a lawyer.

In time, you will offer a publisher a **licence** to publish your novel. You will not offer to hand over the copyright in it. If you are offered a publishing contract in which you are asked to sign away copyright in your novel, rather than grant a licence to publish it in certain territories within a certain time, you should at the very least know the reason why.

when! →

I am still **not** a lawyer.

~~If~~ any of this gets real for you, consult somebody who knows about it for real.

I **am** a member of the Society of Authors, which vets contracts for members. Other organisations are available.

• I can't **not** mention this. Plagiarism. Don't. Not just because sooner or later, somebody's going to find out, but also because it's fundamentally uncreative.

You're not writing if you're copying, but you are stunting your own development (and installing a part that wasn't made for your vehicle - here we go with the metaphors again).

If you like the way a writer handles a scene, feel free to use a similar technique, but with your own words and in your own way. Don't make "it" your own - make your own.

Sooner or later, somebody will tell you that "Talent borrows, genius steals." When he said that, I don't think Oscar Wilde was talking about you.

About the Author

- I've done the product-placement bit, so this doesn't have to be a list of books.

  But what can I say instead of that?

  I know a bit about the book trade.

  I've worked in publishing and journalism. I've read manuscripts, edited books, debated covers and titles, attended meetings about marketing. I've written book reviews and author interviews, back-cover blurbs and, ah, dynamic marketing copy. Next-generation blah-blah.

  Warming to the subject of *Me* - I've been represented by two literary agents in my time, and turned down by one other. I've been published by traditional publishing houses and small presses, fact and fiction, and I've self-published.

  Once in my life, I've had the experience of being met out of the lift by an excited publisher with the words, "It's a bestseller!"

  That's enough, surely?

  I am at least vaguely qualified to write this book.

Let's Make This About You

- Nothing you read, or watch, or follow, or subscribe to, can tell you what's going to work tomorrow.

You know as much as the wisest creative-writing guru about what will succeed next year.

That course you're doing, that podcast, this book you're reading - listen, watch, read, take it all in, but they (we) can only ever talk about what's worked in the past that *might* work in the future. There's no certainty.

If it doesn't feel right to you, don't be told what to do. Follow your instincts.

In writing as in the cheesiest superhero movie, you might as well succeed/fail for what you believe is right.

- You can learn a lot from creative-writing courses, etc., but you can't learn to be you. Learn everything you can, from everywhere, and then write as you. Trust your instincts.

- Write what you want to write. You'll be better at that.

- Develop a habit of being interested in everything. I said that before. But don't automatically seek explanations. See how people behave, watch body language, pick up the 'tells'. It's all research. There are stories all around you.

But if you ever feel a need to understand what's going on around you – try making something up. Tell yourself a story about it. You're in the fiction business, after all, and who's to say the man at the bus stop isn't a visitor from another dimension?

- You can learn a lot from watching a friend read your work. But don't take it to heart. Ask for feedback on completed scenes, not opening sentences and isolated paragraphs.

Asking for feedback on your Opening Sentence is like handing me a detached pedal and asking me whether I like your bicycle.

- See that man over there? He's your reader. How are you going to get him to read your novel? Or that woman? Or that group of youngsters with their skateboards?

Readers are not abstract creatures. They're real people. They're out there. And they want something to read.

Now get back to work.

- Procrastination. I was going to say something about that, wasn't I?

Did you write down the date on which you opened this book about how to start your first novel? You did. Good.

How long ago was that?

Time passes while you're *talking about* writing your first novel.

Time even passes while you're *definitely going* to get round to writing your first novel.

If you opened this book, wrote down the date, read a few pages, thought: interesting exercise; told yourself: I'm *definitely going to get started now,* and then went off and did something else – okay.

But how long ago was that?

I'm just asking.

Getting Published

- Feel free to dream about this. Your options are many and various. You can follow a literary agent's or traditional publisher's submission guidelines, and/or you can do the same with a smaller press. As many times as turns out to be necessary. If you know somebody who knows somebody, you can try that route.

Or you can publish your novel directly via one of the e-book/P.O.D. (Print On Demand) platforms that are available directly to authors. It is possible, because it's been done, to go from self-published to traditionally published. To do that, it helps if you're already selling lots of copies of your novel on your own.

Get the attention of anybody in publishing, and they will want to know how marketable you are. How good your novel is, of course, yes, I was just about to say that, of course, yes, but also, bluntly – will your novel sell?

For an agent or a publisher, the decision to take on a new

author is a decision to commit resources. If your novel looks likely to sell because (let us imagine) you are a celebrity already, or a big-time social-media influencer (are they still a thing?), or some other kind of high-profile person with a lot of followers, you may qualify on that basis as a worthwhile investment.

If your novel looks likely to sell because it's a really good book, but you're not a celebrity, etc., then the question arises: what about you? Are you going to write more novels, and will it therefore be worth investing in building you up as a future big-name author?

The trap is to think of Getting Published as the end-point of the process that you've begun by Getting Started. You can think that way, fine, but writing a novel makes you a writer, and if you're a writer, you write.

This book does not contain a section about marketing, but if potential readers (and publishers) already have access to your writing, they may decide they like it enough to buy your novel.

They gain access to your writing because, as a writer, you write – you blog, you post, you comment, you have a website, you build up a profile. Potential readers know you as a writer even before they get to deciding whether or not they want to add your novel to their cart.

Think of yourself as a Writer. A person who writes novels. And writes a lot else besides.

Because that's what you are.

Further Reading

Read everything.

William Essex lives in
Falmouth, Cornwall, UK.

~~He is the author of~~ He writes.
There's a website – www.williamessex.com

Lightning Source UK Ltd.
Milton Keynes UK
UKHW040626191022
410722UK00004B/116

9 781909 172449